**Bibliographic information published by the German National Library:**

The German National Library lists this publication in the National Bibliography; detailed bibliographic data are available on the Internet at http://dnb.dnb.de .

**Imprint:**

Copyright © 2011 GRIN Verlag, Open Publishing GmbH
Print and binding: Books on Demand GmbH, Norderstedt Germany
ISBN: 978-3-668-04101-1

**This book at GRIN:**

http://www.grin.com/en/e-book/305857/cinema-and-mass-media-in-modernity-walter-benjamin-and-the-reproducible

Cyrus Manasseh

# Cinema and Mass Media in Modernity. Walter Benjamin and the Reproducible Image

GRIN Publishing

**GRIN - Your knowledge has value**

Since its foundation in 1998, GRIN has specialized in publishing academic texts by students, college teachers and other academics as e-book and printed book. The website www.grin.com is an ideal platform for presenting term papers, final papers, scientific essays, dissertations and specialist books.

**Visit us on the internet:**

http://www.grin.com/

http://www.facebook.com/grincom

http://www.twitter.com/grin_com

# 'Cinema and Mass Media in Modernity: Walter Benjamin and the Reproducible Image'

Design Lecture by Dr Cyrus Manasseh PhD Presented C. AUGUST 2011
Presented at the University of Western Sydney, School of Communication Arts, College of Arts, University of Western Sydney

LECTURE NOTES:

## The Power and Impact of Film to Capture Social Events and Mass Change

In fact, we must understand that changing historical understandings of images have been directly influenced by imaging technologies. As we learnt a couple of weeks ago in previous lectures, from the beginning of photography, photographers had always attempted to produce photographs which could be accepted by the same criteria as painting. This was changed however by new people such as Moholy-Nagy, Rodchenko, Man Ray etc. who we already discussed in the tutorials. One of the first theories of film in the English Language was Vachel Lindsay's *The Art of the Moving Picture*, which was published in 1915 which described the motion picture as a great high art. In fact, experiments in Electronic Media had originally begun in 1877 with the sound recordings Edison had made with his cylinder phonograph and the Gramophone (1898) and continuing with radio and silent movies of the 1920s and then talking cinema from 1926 which came out with the Jazz Singer. Following photography and its technological discoveries, Film production would continue to reveal the new link between art and the new developments in science during the early 19th century and the invention of film in the 1890s. Through its system of production, the rules of understanding images changed for everybody in significant ways. This period would be when the new mechanical technologies such as photographic, cinematic, and arriving soon after, television or televisual images would all be infinitely reproducible. This fact would change the role of images in society and greatly increase the influence upon us. In the era of the new films being made from the early 20th century, which had come out of the experiments that were taking place in photography one could say that then motion was added to the photograph. Because of this, early film could in this way be seen as early photoplays and the people best qualified for this had been the painters, architects and sculptors such as Edwin S. Porter in America, Georges Melies in France Dziga Vertov, Sergei Eisenstein in Russia, D.W. Griffith in America who represent some of the most important of these at the time. These new filmmakers were interested in creating a new form and an understanding of beauty, which could replace the previous importance of painting since in many ways, there had been a tendency for many new painters, to avoid representing or reflecting the idea of traditional beauty in painting. However, it was a mechanical process that reproduced in its technical dimension the image and much inherent in Film worked against the concept of authenticity. From this time, the technical attributes of the new medium of film had also meant that an image which had normally been seen just in one context, could now be seen in

1

many many different contexts. This was because Film was able to dissect and manipulate perceptions of reality. This is because of the nature of the film editing process and the "creative" or some might say the "manipulative" nature of editing, which was the discovery that when two shots were joined together the spectator might be made to infer a variety of contrasts and comparisons between two sets of information. By reproducing the image, the filmmaker could unite events which were far apart or divide those which were continuous. It had meant that famous works of art were photographed and filmed and were brought much closer to the public – brought right up close. And images of far places and iconic subjects such as monuments and great masterpieces of art which had only been visible to the public in its original home (that is, one could only see them by visiting the image or the work fact-to-face and in person) were increasingly being made much more immediate and less distant or separated from real life and instead were being brought right into the public's everyday world and therefore daily experience and consciousness. In other words, unique images became localised. Because of this, film could be used to capture and document social events and up to the minute documentation of current events. This brought the public for the very first time and in a completely new way to be able to more closely inspect what was going on in the world from this time. In fact, due to this, images of a distant origin, time and place would now be reproduced in a mass way so that they became more personal – and related to something which could now give the audience the feeling of possessing the idea of the image – which had meant that audiences could almost feel that they possessed their original meaning, essence and the spirit of the work. This helped to create changes in aesthetic style for designers: this is because changes in aesthetic style achieved more than just revealing the history of art and visual culture; it also revealed changes in the development of diverse kinds of world views.

## Debates about the impact of Mechanical Reproduction on Art, Culture & Society

In fact, by 1900 technical reproduction had reached a standard that not only permitted it to reproduce all transmitted works of art and thus to cause the most profound change on the public; it had also captured a place of its own among the artistic processes. In response to this, within the 1930s, debates took place at the time about the impact of mechanical reproduction on art, culture and society that had first begun from the beginning of the 20th century. Walter Benjamin's 1936 essay "The Work of Art in the Age of Mechanical Reproduction" had embodied a wider interest in new cultural forms, which the author had shared with other German intellectuals. For Benjamin, the typical and central new forms of the 20th century had emerged through technologies, which could mass reproduce the image. These were printing, and especially photography and cinema. Benjamin pointed out that there were indeed positive aspects of the mass reproduction of imagery and noted at the time that the mechanical reproduction of art changes the reaction of the masses toward art. He had pointed out that was because individual reactions to mass produced imagery are pre-determined and influenced by their response which is about to be produced (particularly in film). For example, a television news image can be considered valuable because it can be seen simultaneously on many screens at the same time. Benjamin stated that this opens up new possibilities for us all.

However, one of the major points in Benjamin's debate which criticized the usefulness and legitimacy of the new technology such as Film and Cinema which used the reproduced image was that the original aura of the work being photographed and reproduced is lost to reproducibility and that the audience's experiences of the images that were being reproduced from this time forward were not as authentic as they could be if they had experienced the original work itself close at hand and in person; and therefore the quality of the presence of the reproduced image was always depreciated. That is, its essential truth and natural presence and the realness of it, was always lost, or weakened. [1]

Much of the reasoning behind this was based on the fact that an original work before being reproduced by image reproduction technology was truly authentic due to its history as a real object which went back to its origins on the planet to be followed by its duration of life on the planet which legitimized it as something real which contrasted with the newness of a reproduced image of it.

Another issue that had been raised was that a reproduced image of something creates a new context for it to be shown in, which contrasts with how the original work had been before it was reproduced, since it had belonged to a uniquely separate context in which the audience view it – which was usually in a less social or shared or collective experiential way. Therefore, when mass reproduced, instead of a solitary contemplation of the origin work in its previous context, by contrast, the reproduced image of it is characterised by a direct, intimate fusion of visual and emotional enjoyment, which is now combined with the orientation of the expert. It means that individual reactions to mechanically reproduced images makes them conventional and that this makes them uncritically enjoyed and appreciated as if they were something original and real when actually the opposite of this is the case. Instead, a reproduction of an image should be seen as exactly just that, – a reproduction. As Benjamin had stated in relation to the consequences of what could happen in the age of mechanical reproduction:

> "… that which withers in the age of mechanical reproduction is the aura of the work of art. This is a symptomatic process whose significance points beyond the realm of art. One might generalize by saying: the technique of reproduction detaches the reproduced object from the domain of tradition." [2]

In addition, to Film, because of continuing developments in the mass reproduction of imagery which evolved out of evolving new technology, print media from the 1940s would be designed to address a mass audience – a mass public. The 1940s and 1950s saw a time when print media such as picture magazines, newspapers, comic books all came out and comic strip were printed in newspapers. It was when an increasing amount of books – especially those that contained reproduced images such as encyclopaedias, art books and pulp fiction were being published. All of these related to the significance of closely repeatable visual statements which became central to the distribution of new knowledge. From this time, photography, combined with printing, which facilitated all of the new mass production of images used for the above mediums changed the status of the image even further by making it increasingly even more possible to reproduce existing works of art, which had been previously unique.

Yet according to Benjamin's discussion of the loss of the original aura of the work, all of this would make the image lose its true authenticity and I would definitely agree with him on this. He wrote that even the most perfect reproduction of a work of art is lacking in one element: its presence in time and space, its unique existence at the place where it happens to be.[3]

However, this problem of authenticity was carried even further by the new development of electronic media which gained enormous momentum from the 1960s with analogue video reproduction and then digital reproductions.

SLIDE 1: Shows an image of mechanisation; assembly-line mass production.

SLIDE 2: Shows 2 images of mechanisation's impact on human labour and bodies: linear, rhythmic, repetitive, fast-speeds.

SLIDE 3: Shows an image of mass manufacturing in a factory.

SLIDE 4: Shows another image of mass manufacturing in a factory.

In relation to slides 1-4, all the mass production which had begun during the industrial revolution – which was central to it, was now being combined with the idea of reproducing images of the original work or the original image so that it could and therefore would become mass produced.

This mass production of images and imagery would continue to increase right up to today with the aura dissolved of the original object which had been reproduced in mass imagery through its being photographed or filmed.

This repeats the problem or the question of authenticity of the reproduced image in comparison with the original work or image being photographed, filmed and reproduced many times in books, cinema, and in advertising in the media especially on television which is designed to hypnotise its audiences through its ongoing broadcast of mass reproduced imagery.

However, notwithstanding this, the concept of authenticity is used in many different ways today. For example, advertising and the media such its commercials have very very often claimed that what it is advertising including everything it says about the product and what it associates with the product including the kind of people using the product being sold in the commercial is actually authentic when it is not – when they are not. Often as a way to manipulate the public into buying a product, commercials use jerky amateur camera work and natural sound and lighting to create a realist effect, selling the idea that nothing in the ad has been orchestrated or faked, and references to tradition are used to sell identities that cannot be acquired simply by purchasing a product. Yet, its common value by a mass audience (that is almost everyone who watches television) feels themselves to be individuals watching or reading magazines who believe that what they see on television or read in magazines is authentic and therefore true when this is actually the opposite of what is actually true. Authenticity means genuine, reliable, not false or copied. This is what Benjamin was correctly pointing out in 1936.

Therefore, we have to realise that we now live in a society that is absolutely filled with images of this kind and it had begun from this period of early modernism, in the early $20^{th}$ century, when the images began to be mass reproduced by photography, film and print media.

During the time, in 1929 in order to make the reproduction of images more authentic or seem to be more authentic or to argue that the reproduced/ photographed image can be authentic the Russian experimental filmmaker Dziga Vertov made an important film.

SLIDE 5: *Man with a Movie Camera* (1929).

The film *Man with a Movie Camera* is a documentary about life in the city in the Soviet Union during a period of modernization. Viewing the film the audience is made conscious of the process involved in filming due to the different techniques used by the cameraman such as freeze frames, split screens, various montages, dissolves and slow motion all of which exhibit the director's new vision of the changing world. Yet it was these techniques that have become the essential tools and elements of film experimentation and by extension, the filming and production of advertising commercials.

SLIDE 6: The Russian film director Dziga Vertov wrote:

"I am an eye. A Mechanical eye. I, the machine, show you a world the way only I can see it. I free myself for today and forever from human immobility. I'm in constant movement. I approach and pull away from objects. I creep under them. I move alongside a running horse's mouth. I fall and rise with the falling and rising bodies…."[4]

SLIDE 7: Vertov also wrote:

> "Film drama is the opium of the people… down with bourgeois fairy-tale scenarios…long live life as it is."[5]

SLIDE 8: Vertov's focus on the impacts of mechanisation has influenced many filmmakers: Two recent films that have explored montage techniques to record life and aspects of mechanisation are *Baraka* and *Koyaanisquatsi*.

Vertov's films and his writings show that he was interested in revealing the reality of modern life which was about mechanization.

SLIDE 9: Shows an Image of Walter Benjamin.

SLIDE 10: Walter Benjamin "The Work of Art in the Age of Mechanical Reproduction" (1936).

Questions Benjamin's text raise for us are:

o Has the aura of the original declined in the wake of mechanical reproductions?
o To what extent have the technologies of film and photography opened up new experiences to audiences?
o To what extent have they opened up our perceptions to things which were previously unconscious?
o Can photography and film bring about the possibility of mass social change?

SLIDE 11: Has the aura of the original declined in the wake of mechanical reproductions?

SLIDE 12: Shows the Original Painting of Leonardo Da Vinci's Mona Lisa.

SLIDE 13: Shows an Image of Someone Photographing the Painting of Leonardo Da Vinci's Mona Lisa in a Gallery with a lot of people around.

SLIDE 14: Shows an Image of Modern Pop Icon/Juxtaposed Side by Side with another Photo of Da Vinci's Mona Lisa with a Simpsons Head.

SLIDE 15: Image of Leonardo Da Vinci's Mona Lisa used in an Advertisement to sell food.

SLIDE 16: To what extent have the technologies of film and photography opened up new experiences to audiences? To what extent have they opened up our perceptions to things which were previously unconscious or invisible?

SLIDE 17: Shows an Image of Leonardo Da Vinci's Mona Lisa as a Manipulated Image.

SLIDE 18: *"Our eyes see very little and very badly – so people dreamed up the microscope to let them see invisible phenomena; they invented the telescope…now they have perfected the cinecamera to penetrate more deeply into the visible world, to explore and record visual phenomena so that what is happening now, which will have to be taken account of in the future, is not forgotten."* (Vertov)

SLIDE 19: Can photography and film bring about the possibility of mass social change?

**SLIDE 20: Summary of historical context that informs Benjamin's essay:**

1) The Nazi's used mass media to seduce, marshal, indoctrinate, control, and dominate the German people into a mass of supporters. Mechanical reproduction – film, photography, radio – allowed a mass audience to come "face to face with themselves."

2) The Nazi Party aestheticised politics; the design of mass spectacles gave their politics an attractive and spectacular face. This can be seen in Leni Riefenstahl's film "The Triumph of the Will." (1934)

SLIDE 21:
3) Benjamin was critical of Fascism, claiming it was preventing an opportunity for the masses to effect social change and alter property relations in the 1930s in favour of a better distribution of wealth. According to Benjamin mechanical reproduction like film and photography seemed to represent a disruption of the aura or authenticity of art. Benjamin believed that this disruption of the aura, was an opportunity to produce non-elitist and accessible art forms by the people and to effect social change.

4) Fascism according to Benjamin was not giving people their right to social change. The people were only being given a chance to participate in their own organisation as art; a nationalistic, pseudo-religious and ritualistic art-form. He anticipated that this activity would lead to war not revolution.

SLIDE 22: Shows Scenes from Leni Riefenstahl's *Triumph of the Will* – 1934.

SLIDE 23: Shows Examples of John Heartfield's political photomontage: Propaganda: Photomontage used as a tool to generate social change.

SLIDES 24-28: Shows Examples of John Heartfield's Photo Montage.

# Notes

[1] Walter Benjamin, *"The Work of Art in Age of Mechanical Reproduction"*, 1936, http://www.berk-edu.com/VisualStudies/readingList/06b_benjamin-

[2] Walter Benjamin, *"The Work of Art in Age of Mechanical Reproduction"*, 1936, http://www.berk-edu.com/VisualStudies/readingList/06b_benjamin-work%20of%20art%20in%20the%20age%20of%20mechanical%20reproduction.pdf

[3] Walter Benjamin, *"The Work of Art in Age of Mechanical Reproduction"*, 1936, http://www.berk-edu.com/VisualStudies/readingList/06b_benjamin-work%20of%20art%20in%20the%20age%20of%20mechanical%20reproduction.pdf

[4] Dziga Vertov, *Kino-Eye: the Writings of Dziga Vertov* (translated by Kevin O'Brien), Berkeley, University of California Press, 1984.

[5] Dziga Vertov, *Kino-Eye: the Writings of Dziga Vertov* (translated by Kevin O'Brien), Berkeley, University of California Press, 1984.